Angela-
Believe

Hold Your Breath

Make A Wish

Count To Three

And Come With Me

To

The World
of
JAKE BELIEVE!

JAKE JACOBSON

Dedication

One of the privileges of writing a book is the opportunity to offer a page of dedication.

Certainly, I acknowledge my wife Debbie, of more than four decades, and we are the original Mr. & Mrs. Lucky, our amazing sons, Alex & Ari, and our perfect daughter-in law, Sara. As well, a most dear friend...and he knows who he is, and an array of business associates and customers who over these many years have allowed me to be a part of their plan.

For all of them, I am grateful and I thank them.

But as I read the final draft of this book, I have realized that this book is not about my experience or my past. It's about my future.

It's about your future. And the future of everyone who has a thirst to view this world through rose colored glasses and who reaches for the stars with unbridled desire for success.

And there's no one that I can think of who better represents that very positive attitude than our year and a half old grandson EMMETT, who with every step he takes and with every sound he makes, he does so with endless wonder, and in constant reach of success with a smile.

Thanks for the lesson, EMMETT. This one's for you.
Love, GRANDPA JAKE

Forward

Aa a young boy, I suffered from terrible case of stuttering. Through my entire process of grade school, at every family function and at every attempt to even speak my own name, my obvious disability caused me to be socially awkward, perpetually embarrassed and frustrated beyond explanation.

My parents arranged for speech therapy, my elementary school placed me in the "special" class and my brother and sister would try to help by finishing my sentences. Bad idea.

Actually, nothing worked.

Until, one day, at the age of 14, I decided to get a job...as a TELEPHONE SOLICITOR!

That's right! A telephone solicitor!

Five nights a week, I would sit in a "boiler room" with other solicitors in a room of divided privacy walls and would call people soliciting customers for a home improvement company.

On the wall in front of me was a one-page script that I was told to simply read, word for word, to everyone that answered. That script was designed as questions about what their next project might be.

In the middle of the room was a cardboard box with a bunch of cut up pages from the telephone book. This was our call list.

And in the back of the room was a bulletin board decorated as a horse race with each solicitor's name attached to one of the horses. Whenever one of our set appointments resulted in an actual in home estimate, the horse advanced and when they became sales, they advanced more. Who ever was ahead at the end of the week got a $2.00 bonus!

And it was those three ideas that I learned in my new, young career teaching me three valuable lessons that I still live by today. Amongst other lessons that I've learned over the years, I've shaped my own success in training others, managing others, developing selling systems and personally selling well over a million dollars each year.

The first thing I remember is that written script. Amazingly, I learned at a very early age that a rehearsed script allowed me to be comfortable in what I was saying and more importantly that I could control the conversations. I LEARNED THAT QUESTIONS CONTROL.

Next was that list of names out of the phonebook. It became very obvious to me that whoever made the most calls, got the most leads and whoever got the most leads got the most sales.

I LEARNED THAT IT'S A NUMBERS GAME

And last but not least was that horse race on the bulletin board.

I'm not sure that I was chasing the $2.00 bonus, but I am sure that I wanted to WIN. I learned that I LOVE THE GAME BEYOND THE SCORE.

And since that time, I've always worked and lived by those three lessons...and more that I've learned along the way. And, that I still learn every day.

This book relates those lessons and more that I've learned and over these 50 plus years and have been proven to be valuable ideas that work. And in my world of success, I believe in these lessons and in the idea of a structured selling system engineered by discipline, consistency, and a positive attitude. Today, I am a successful salesperson and a successful sales trainer. I do what I like and like what I do. I make a good living.

It's a pretty good feeling to be a part of such a plan.

And I no longer stutter.

I'm Jake...
AND IN MY WORLD...
I BELIEVE THAT...

Success Is Premeditated

Success is the result of a planned, structured and rehearsed system. And that includes a selling system. Not by quick reaction, uneducated guesses and not by the gift of gab.

Find or design a plan...and follow it. In other words, follow the yellow brick road....why wouldn't you? Word has it that a systemized strategy works. Trust me. It does. Over the years, I've made a very good living by simply following the yellow brick road. And I've lived happily very after.

I'm Jake...
AND IN MY WORLD...
I BELIEVE THAT...

A Positive Attitude Is A Real Step To Success

Positive thinking not only leads to a successful process....it also offers the probability of a successful outcome. Far better than a negative attitude which coincidently stacks the odds against you and actually roadmaps failure. Simple enough. So don't complicate it by thinking anything but positive. Create your own offensive huddle and play the game with the attitude to WIN.

I'm Jake...
AND IN MY WORLD...
I BELIEVE THAT...

If You're Not Prepared,
You're Gonna F*ck It Up

Being unprepared not only diminishes your chances of success...

It also shows with transparent evidence that you can't be trusted, believed or even liked, all of which are necessary for success. A bad first impression rarely ends well. How dumb would it be to ruin your own destiny? Really.

I'm Jake...
AND IN MY WORLD...
I BELIEVE THAT...

They Will Tell You How To Sell Them...
IF YOU LISTEN

Often, a prospect will reveal their needs or desires and even their buying habits, methods or hints on how to satisfy their own hopes that you could be the answer to those needs. So let'em talk....and listen. It works. Trust me.

I'm Jake...
AND IN MY WORLD...
I BELIEVE THAT...

People Would Rather Buy
Then Be Sold

Without a doubt, everyone would rather feel like they decided to buy than to feel like forced into it by a fast-talking salesperson. A good sign in knowing that they really do feel good about everything is when they tell you "write it up".

So, as per their idea....."write it up". And oh yeah, CA-CHING!

I'm Jake...
AND IN MY WORLD...
I BELIEVE THAT...

First Sell,
Then Close

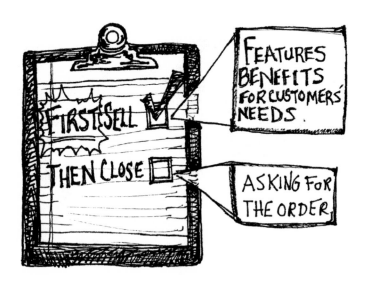

Selling and closing are TWO DIFFERENT actions.

Selling is highlighting the features and benefits of the product or service, the good reputation of the company and the affordability of the project...and meeting the customer's needs or wants.

Closing is simply asking for the order. And you gotta' do both. And, by the way. First sell, then close. It's amazing how many times I've seen salespeople try to start closing right away. Wrong method. Trust me.

I'm Jake...
AND IN MY WORLD...
I BELIEVE THAT...

If You Don't Think You're Going To Make The Sale, Don't Go

All of my salespeople know my policy that if they are driving to the appointment and talking themselves out of making the sale by thinking negative, also known as "stinkin thinkin", they need to call me so that I can redirect them back to their own house and re-issue the appointment to a winner. If you don't think you're good enough to succeed, you're not.

I'm Jake...
AND IN MY WORLD...
I BELIEVE THAT...

Salesman Sell
And
Customers Buy

And it's important to know the difference. Follow your given role as the seller and if you follow the system which should include questions that you know the answers to, you can lead your customer prospect toward the role of buying and becoming a customer. Play your role and let them play their's.

Pretty cool, huh?

I'm Jake...
AND IN MY WORLD...
I BELIEVE THAT...

You Should Do What You Like And Like What You Do. Really.

Those guys from the LIFE IS GOOD® company got it right. And why not? Why would anyone want to do what they don't like to do? And the answer that suggests that it's "for the money" is a bad reason and short lived.

Satisfaction, smiles and enjoyment is always better than the alternatives. Every day. Every time. Guaranteed.

I'm Jake...
AND IN MY WORLD...
I BELIEVE THAT...

Questions Control

Without a doubt, you have more control over anyone by simply asking questions. As humans, we are all preconditioned to respond to questions and the answers you get can reveal the answers you need or want. Build your presentation around questions and you win. Just think about the fact that if your customers asked all the questions, you would constantly be on the defensive mode. And if that is happening, you lose. Every time. Guaranteed.

I'm Jake...
AND IN MY WORLD...
I BELIEVE THAT...

You Should Make It About THEM

Customers don't care what products you have in your house, what colors you like or what you think they should buy. Design every conversation about THEM and not only will they appreciate it, but the scales of success are leaned toward the idea that it's more about the customer than you. And yes, this actually reads in your favor. And by the way, what they appreciate is your advice, not your opinion.

Experience offers the comfort of trust and knowledge. Opinions are all about you and nobody really cares.

I'm Jake...
AND IN MY WORLD...
I BELIEVE THAT...

It's Not About Price
It's About Value

IF YOU DON'T BELIEVE THIS,
RETURN THIS BOOK FOR A REFUND

I don't believe in "Born Salesmen". Such ego minded fast talkers miss a lot, including the fact that what people buy is VALUE, not price. And when they don't sell, they themselves blame it on the idea that "our prices must be too high" rather than to BUILD VALUE. As well, those who tout their careers as being able to sell ice to those who live in igloos, are in my world, also con artists. Short sighted, short success and short-lived careers.

Actually, it's NOT about the price. What customers want is not the cheapest product. They want the best product for the best deal. So, don't sell price. Sell Value. Thinking cheap is a bad plan for the customer...and for you.

I'm Jake...

AND IN MY WORLD...
I BELIEVE THAT...

You Should try EVERYTHING...
You'll Never See Them Again

No matter what, if a customer promises to call you tomorrow and gives you his wallet to hold, it's not his wallet.

He's not calling you tomorrow. He's either doubting the value, the affordability, the product, the company, or you. And once you leave and take your suggestion of emotions with you, it's over. I strongly suggest that you do not go home and tell your significant other to order that new sofa because the guy promised to call you back. He's not.

I'm Jake...
AND IN MY WORLD...
I BELIEVE THAT...

It's A Numbers Game

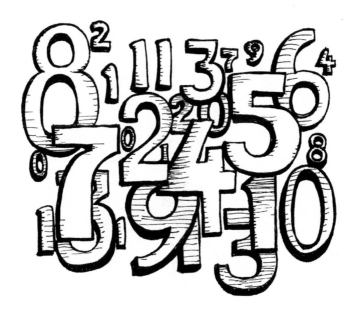

No doubt, the profession of selling is a numbers game. The more leads you run, the more presentations you make. And the more presentations you make, the more sales you will make. The last time I checked, if you run 1 appointment on any given day, you probably won't make 2 sales. Beyond being prepared and processing an entire selling system, improve your odds by increasing the numbers. A lot. Math adds up.

In other words, work hard.

I'm Jake...
AND IN MY WORLD...
I BELIEVE THAT...

EMPATHY SELLS
NOT SYMPATHY

One of the biggest mistakes a sales rep makes on a sales call is to offer sympathy when a customer describes a previous bad experience or the familiar claim of "sticker shock". Sympathy might suggest that you feel bad for the customer and that won't get you sales.

Empathy, however, will offer you the natural follow up of suggesting that you understand the customer and will also suggest your position of putting yourself in their position. Don't feel bad for them. Help them feel better.

Smart move. They'll appreciate it and so will your accountant.

I'm Jake...
AND IN MY WORLD...
I BELIEVE THAT...

Auto University Is A Great Institution

After more than 50 years in the business, I must admit that I'm more on top of my game than I've ever been...And I will also tell you it's because I actually drive to my appointments and still listen to the likes of world-renowned Zig Ziglar and one of my favorite authors, Harvey Mackay. And it doesn't have to be new material. It's a reminder for me to hold the bat right, check my batting stance and to take the proper swing. You'd be surprised at how much you can re-learn.

I'm Jake...
AND IN MY WORLD...
I BELIEVE THAT...

You Should Arrive At A 6PM Appointment
At EXACTLY 6PM

Not at 5:55, not at 6:30 and no, not at 6:01.

Being early might deprive the customer of that final bite of dinner, time to do the dishes or the time to relax before your appointment.

Late is absolutely inexcusable, suggests to the customer that now everyone in your company will be late...and that you don't respect their time and that you consider yours more important.

Arriving at exactly the right time is smart. Early or late, isn't. It's stupid.

I'm Jake...
AND IN MY WORLD...
I BELIEVE THAT...

Pre- Judging
Is A VERY BAD IDEA

First of all, you never know what you have to work with until you see what's on the other of the door. Pre-judging because of customer's names, neighborhoods, hoarding habits or anything else will only help accomplish your secret desire to make it a quick sales call. So, go ahead. Pre-judge. And then you can go home early.

I'm Jake...
AND IN MY WORLD...
I BELIEVE THAT...

You're on Stage
So, Rehearse

If you want to be a successful sales rep, arrive the same way, warm up the same way, measure the same way, demo the same way, close the same way, EVERY TIME!

That way, it always sounds complete, confident and impressive to the customer (and yourself) . Consistency assures the accuracy of the selling system...and again, the same system every time.

And yes, practice.... Every sports hero, actor, musician, military service person, medical professional, teacher, and every other accomplished winner in life practices, even when they think they know it all. Show everyone that you are a winner that you know you are...and you will become one.

I'm Jake...
AND IN MY WORLD...
I BELIEVE THAT...

When You Don't Sell,
They Are Just As Disappointed As You Are

Driving home from an appointment without a sale sucks, Right? Well, guess what, the customer is just as disappointed as you are. Believe me when I tell you that the only reason you went to the appointment was to sell the job...and the only reason that they made the appointment was to satisfy a need or a desire....by buying! A "NO SALE" is a double loss.

Remember that buying is an emotional decision and that the fizzle of not buying is a much sadder feeling than the sizzle of signing on the dotted line. Go for the sizzle.

I'm Jake...

AND IN MY WORLD...
I BELIEVE THAT...

You Should Never Chase Money.
Let Money Follow YOU

One of the biggest temptations is to count your commission while you're selling. If you are doing this... STOP!

The profession of selling indeed can and should result in HIGH PAY, but the top producers focus not on their next paycheck, but rather, their next sale.

And big paychecks are because of lots of sales. Not just one big sale. Consistency increases success.

And sales are not made because of paychecks. Paychecks are made because of sales .....along with your hard work, your smart work and your dedication to your profession. Get that straight.

I'm Jake...

AND IN MY WORLD...

I BELIEVE THAT...

When You Sell
And They Buy
You Are Helping People

That's right. You are helping people realize their needs or desires. You are helping people save energy and money with new energy saving products and you are helping them protect their largest investment with a new roof and increasing the value. Feel good about that. You should. And thank you. Take a bow!

I'm Jake...

AND IN MY WORLD...

I BELIEVE THAT...

OUTRUN THE BEAR

Nope. No need to.

Good lesson in life. There are two guys in the woods and one notices a bear. In a panic, he suggests that they need to outrun the bear. "Wrong" answers his friend..."I just have to out run you." You don't have to compete with the customer's 49 other quotes. You just have to sell them on your proposal. The others don't matter.

And a bonus point. If your quote is $7,000 and they have another quote for $5,000...you don't need to make a $7,000 sale...you just need to make a $2000. sale.

The finish line is closer than you think.

I'm Jake...
AND IN MY WORLD...
I BELIEVE THAT...

If You Don't Ask For The Order…
You Won't Get It.

It's great to be knowledgeable or to do a great job at demonstrating the product. But you've also got to ask for the order. And I mean REALLY ask.

If you don't, they'll simply thank you for your time and promise to call you later. Don't hold your breath. Like my mother used to tell me, you'll turn blue. Simply, if you don't ask, you won't get. What a shame. And to think...you were the one that made such a bad decision.

I'm Jake...
AND IN MY WORLD...
I BELIEVE THAT...

Before You Ask Them To Invest
You Should Invest
In Yourself

Investing in yourself is smart. Partake in seminars, self-help books, ride-alongs with your Sales Manager, positive attitude books, a new car, a new brief case... whatever you can do to make YOU better. You deserve it.

And, if your prospects notice (and they will) that you're invested in the process, so will they. People follow winners.

I'm Jake...
AND IN MY WORLD...
I BELIEVE THAT...

You're In A Selling Situation…
Not A Race…

I'm in every one of my sales call for exactly 2 ½ hours. Every call. Every time.

That's my system and that's my rehearsed role. Those who tell me that they can sell in under one hour leave me unimpressed with a known likelihood that the job will cancel because of questioned value that was poorly presented in a rushed hurry. If you don't have the time to stay, don't go. Rushing through any process is a transparent message to your customer that what you're saying isn't important. Stupid is as stupid does on your part.

A guaranteed loss.

I'm Jake...
AND IN MY WORLD...
I BELIEVE THAT...

SELLING IS A CONVERSATION

One of my favorite sayings is "Selling Is A Conversation." They just might tell you something. You just might tell them something.

Make sure everybody talks.

Make sure everybody listens.

It's a good plan.

I'm Jake...
AND IN MY WORLD...
I BELIEVE THAT...

THE CUSTOMER IS YOUR COMPETITION

True story. After a full demonstration and price presentation to an interested customer, I was offered the typical "I'll be getting other estimates" response... to which I responded, "From whom"?

The customer then responded..." Good question....I'm not sure....Tell me, Jake...who's your competition?"

My response..." YOU ARE!"

I'd rather worry about something within my control...like my customer...rather than the ABC Company down the street.

By the way, the customer loved that answer. The sale was made. And I loved the commission.

I'm Jake...
AND IN MY WORLD...
I BELIEVE THAT...

Selling Is the Transference Of Belief

It is of the utmost importance that you truly believe in yourself, your company, and your product. And I mean that sincerely. And sincerity itself is so transparent that a customer can see right through your disbelief. A good reality check here is to step back and consider.... In your opinion, beyond your obvious earning a commission, should your customer make the decision to buy? If you believe they should...it'll show. I wonder what happens when you believe that they shouldn't buy?

I'm Jake...
AND IN MY WORLD...
I BELIEVE THAT...

Making Them Accountable
Works

Simply and definitely, if a customer says that they are getting another estimate, ask them from who, what day and what time. If they say that they are deciding on Thursday, ask them what's gonna happen between today and Thursday. In other words, make them accountable for every statement.

You need those answers and often, they need to hear themselves say those words. So ask them. Let them talk. Let them listen to what they just said. Sometimes, that means more.

THIS WORKS

I'm Jake...
AND IN MY WORLD...
I BELIEVE THAT...

You Should
LET THEM WIN

By human nature, buyers are preconditioned to want to get a good deal, not to be given a good deal. In other words, to them buying is a game. And, more than anything, despite details of reality or the actual idea of the best deal, they want to win. And while I'm not suggesting any less than a truthful and full disclosure, LET THEM WIN. And they're entitled to win. They're paying YOU.

As the loser in this game of negotiation, you get the honorable mention...of going to the bank....and if you're smart, on a regular basis.

I'm Jake...
AND IN MY WORLD...
I BELIEVE THAT...

IT IS WHAT IT IS
IS WHAT IT IS

Let it be known that I keep a rock on my desk with this very saying engraved on it. And it's because I believe it and live each day by its intention of meaning.

Rather than question the facts that surround us, accepting them is not only a better idea, but it affords us the advantage of falling in line with what is actually happening or what is actually evident.

Those who question or challenge the company's policy, the procedures as outlined or the methods of doing business the "company way" will ultimately get exactly what they deserve... a headache... or at the minimum, get a false sense of temporary success, aka.... a real sense of failure.

I'm Jake...
AND IN MY WORLD...
I BELIEVE THAT...

You Should Keep Your Experience In Your Back Pocket

Anytime I interview a prospective sales rep, I'm very clear to advise them that if they have worked for another company that utilizes different procedures, pricing guidelines or other "we used to" methods, that they should keep that experience in his back pocket.

Realizing past experience may be valuable if thought of as a foundation of building upon one's past, It can also prevent you from accepting the current process or maybe, even worse, can prevent you from learning.

And that is a most valuable lesson. I guarantee it.

I'm Jake...
AND IN MY WORLD...
I BELIEVE THAT...

The Harder You Work, The Luckier You Get

I can't tell you how many times I've worked all day and driven all over God's country only to go home empty handed without any new contracts to process. And then, the next morning, lo and behold, a long-forgotten prospect from months ago calls the office to say that they've decided to proceed with the job. Actually, it's not luck, it's just because you're being rewarded for hard work. And luck is rewarded to those who deserve it. Earned benefits.

I'm Jake...
AND IN MY WORLD...
I BELIEVE THAT...

When You Make A Sale, Don't Say THANK YOU…
Say
Congratulations
AND THEY WILL SAY
THANK YOU

That's right. Anytime you say "thank you" to a customer, you're thanking them for your commission.

By congratulating them, you're actually making them feel good about their decision to buy.

And in response to your compliment, they will thank you for not only the compliment but for helping them to get such a good deal and for working with them.

As they should. Pretty smart, huh?

I'm Jake...
AND IN MY WORLD...
I BELIEVE THAT...

You Should Under Promise And Over Deliver

Bad news. One of the challenges in selling is meeting the true unknown level of expectation...and by virtue of the fact that it was you who promises them absolute happiness, I strongly suggest that you limit your liability of disappointment. And, there's good news...You can and will also score some additional brownie points by surprising them with better expectations than they might have expected.

Choose your game plan, your words and your delivery of promises. Wisely, carefully and intentionally.

I'm Jake...
AND IN MY WORLD...
I BELIEVE THAT...

You Should Not Undersell
And You Should Not Oversell

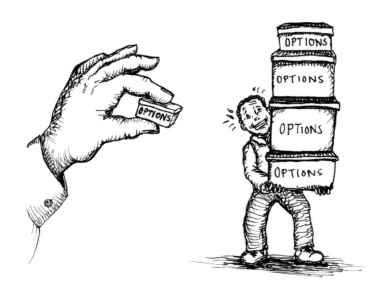

On a one call close, you need to develop a single offering to your customer. Too many options will result in indecision.

That being said, be sure to decide on the proper scope of the project. Some customers would rather do everything at once, others might feel better doing the job in stages. Either way, based on YOUR LISTENING to the customers' conversation....don't try to oversell,...nor undersell.

By the way, you don't need to be a psychic here, just a good listener.

I'm Jake...
AND IN MY WORLD...
I BELIEVE THAT...

You Should NEVER Count Your Commission
While You Are On A Sales Call

I have actually witnessed salespeople (while on ride alongs) actually count and write down their commission on their clipboard while pricing the job.

Bad move. For more than one reason.

Assuming that you don't want you customer to only concentrate on the money, nor should you. Do it, and they can tell.

As well, never chase money. Let money follow you. You'll be surprised at how much you make at the end of the week.

I'm Jake...
AND IN MY WORLD...
I BELIEVE THAT...

They Would Rather Know That You Care
Than Care What You Know

As I've said before, empathy sells. Not sympathy.

When you are LISTENING to the customer's needs or wants (the two reasons why people buy), show that you care. Repeat their concerns to them in confirming that you've heard and care what they just told you.

And this could include every single word or concern. Let them know that you're listening! To Everything!

And be careful not to put yourself on such a high podium above the necessary positioning of experience and work ethic.

Simply touting how much you know diminishes the connection that you need when they are making a decision on whether to buy or not. People don't like "know- it- alls".

I'm Jake...
AND IN MY WORLD...
I BELIEVE THAT...

Selling Is A SYSTEM
GET ONE-LEARN ONE-USE ONE
EVERY TIME

Just like the step by step instruction sheet included with bookshelves pur-
chased at IKEA, I believe that selling is a system, not a talent. A step by step
system that is followed every time, on every sales call. By following the same
system every time, by demo-ing your product the same way every time, by
using the same warm up process every time...etc, etc....every time.....you will:

Get proficient at the presentation

Present yourself with confidence

Include everything without omission every time

Get better at selling..every time

I'm Jake...
AND IN MY WORLD...
I BELIEVE THAT...

Good Things Happen When You Lead An Ace

In the world of gambling, the best card is an ACE. And in the world of selling, you should always lead with the ACE. Set the stage that you are performing on and highlight all those great features...as well as those great benefits that your customer will realize.

It's a good idea to let your prospect know that you offer quality products at fair prices and that you're proud to be in partnership with success.

Play a strong hand. And play to win.

I'm Jake...
AND IN MY WORLD...
I BELIEVE THAT...

You Should Go Tailgating

I consider myself to be a professional salesman, a professional sales trainer and a professional tailgater. And I do it all with passion, with preparation and with belief of success.

And, whether I'm selling for my company, training a new rep or wearing the proud color of Baltimore RAVENS purple...I'm rooting for the home team. So should YOU.

Not a bad way to spend the day.

I'm Jake...
AND IN MY WORLD...
I BELIEVE THAT...

Before You Go Into A Sales Call
LEAVE YOUR AGGRAVATION OUTSIDE

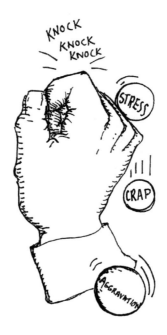

And you can. And you HAVE TO! Whether you are married and feel the stress of obligations of home life, challenged with a financial issue or find yourself otherwise thinking about other crap...you need to leave that crap outside.

Really leave it outside. Literally. When you arrive at the house, KNOCK ON THE DOOR (as opposed to ringing the door bell)... And when you do, envision your aggravation actually rolling and watching it fall to the ground.

It'll be there when you come out, but don't take it inside on a sales call with you. Just think about selling. In my world, I'm thinking success.

I'm Jake...
AND IN MY WORLD...
I BELIEVE THAT...

You Should Practice Your Presentation Before You Get There.
Not In Front Of The Customer

Sound elementary? It is. But you'd be surprised how many sales reps fumble when looking for available options in the catalog, break the glass while trying to tilt in a window sample or have no idea where to find a price on what has been laid out for him in the office and ready for easy access. But you 'gotta practice. Really. If you think that it looks or feels stupid to practice in front of your wife, the mirror, or the family dogs (could be ruff critics) it'll look even worse if your practice in front of your customers...who will then probably opt out of being your guinea pig of purchasing. Of course, the dog probably won't hold you accountable for all the answers, but chances are the customers will be... so avoid 'ruff critics.

I'm Jake...
AND IN MY WORLD...
I BELIEVE THAT...

The Word "BUT"
IS A VERY BAD WORD

Whenever you use the word " but", you are suggesting a complete and rude ignorance of what your customer just said, as well as what you just said.

Customer: "I already have a quote and that door was $500. Cheaper..."

You: "Yes, BUT, Mrs. Jones, our product is better, because..."

You just IGNORED THE FACT THAT SHE SPOKE!

A better word: AND...

AND, Mrs Jones, our product has a stronger frame and that's why it cost more...

NOW, the customer can and will make a decision on both your information AND their input. BY AVOIDING THE WORD "BUT", everything that is said matters. And it does.

I'm Jake...
AND IN MY WORLD...
I BELIEVE THAT...

You Need To Manage
Your Time
Your Money
Your Emotions

Whether you are an employee, contractor or independent, as a salesman you need to control your own destiny. You really do write your own work ethic, your own schedule and your own paycheck.

And, as a self operator, you need to be able to manage your own money, your own schedule...and your own emotions. It's up to YOU to budget. It's up to YOU not to miss appointments or opportunities and it's solely YOUR own decision to get angry over the petty crap that other people inject into your world. I'm not suggesting that co workers, relatives and other idiots don't operate within our arenas, but I am pointing out that it is your decision to let it bother you. Hint: DON'T COUNT THE AMOUNT OF ITEMS THAT THE LADY IN FRONT OF YOU IN THE 10 OR LESS AISLE HAS IN HER SHOPPING CART. If she has 11, and you know it because you counted them....well, that was your decision.

I'm Jake...
AND IN MY WORLD...
I BELIEVE THAT...

IT'S YOUR DECISION that you got mad
And that was stupid

Actually, the belief as listed above was so good, I thought I'd repeat it.

Read it again.

Then, practice it.

I'm Jake...
AND IN MY WORLD...
I BELIEVE THAT...

They Don't Care That You Use The Product

I've never been impressed by salesmen who lie to customers that they have the same product in their house. Or by the salesman who actually do have the product and think that the customer should therefore buy the product just because you have it. You're wrong. They don't care what you have. It's about them.

Sell your experience. Not what you have. It's not about you.

I'm Jake...
AND IN MY WORLD...
I BELIEVE THAT...

EVERYDAY Offers
The Experience Of Yesterday, The Opportunity Of Today
And The Promise Of Tomorrow

Definition: Learn every day. And when you do, do it with a positive attitude. Realize what you either excelled at or underperformed at yesterday.

Approach today with a YES I CAN attitude.

And no matter what...YES, Tomorrow has promises and possibilities beyond your dreams. And your dreams matter.

I'm Jake...
AND IN MY WORLD...
I BELIEVE THAT...

People Don't Buy Features
They Buy Benefits

Keep in mind when you are selling or presenting the parts and pieces of your product, that each part is a "feature". For example, the window that you are selling may tilt in. And that, is a feature.

The "benefit" of that feature is that it makes it easy to clean.

And people buy benefits. Not features.

And good salespeople highlight those benefits that hit the customer's hot buttons...the ones that they told you about...if you listened.

I'm Jake...
AND IN MY WORLD...
I BELIEVE THAT...

You Should
EMPTY THE TRUNK

As part of training, I give all of my new reps samples to show to the customers. Window samples, door samples, parts kits, etc.

While demonstrating and presenting these products, be sure to EMPTY YOUR TRUNK and to use every sample and parts kit that goes with the product line. In other words, DON'T LEAVE THE HEAT LAMP IN YOUR CAR. Use it! Lazy doesn't sell.

Show the demonstration and INVOLVE THE CUSTOMER. When presenting all the parts, LEAVE EVERYTHING IN PLAIN VIEW ON THE TABLE. And when you're done, DON'T PUT ANYTHING AWAY.

Allow the customers the privilege of touching what they're buying and if they don't buy, allow them the disappointment of watching their dreams go away.

This leaves the customer in the desire mode until you put everything away.... that is, until you are writing up the contract... and bonus tip here...., if they don't buy, they will be disassembling their dream.

I'm Jake...
AND IN MY WORLD...
I BELIEVE THAT...

You Should
HIT THE HOT BUTTONS

Simple, specific and important.

When a customer tells you early that they are interested in new windows because their energy bills are too high, be sure to HIGHLIGHT the feature of double pane glass with energy efficient glass.

HIT THEIR HOT BUTTON

This DOES NOT MEAN that you should not show ALL of the features and benefits...I'm suggesting that you HIT THE TARGET they have already revealed to you...if you listened.

I'm Jake...
AND IN MY WORLD...
I BELIEVE THAT...

You Should
KNOW WHAT YOU ARE GOING TO SAY
BEFORE YOU SAY IT

A good lawyer knows what he's going to say before he says it...and often knows the answer to the question that he's about to ask. Actors on stage know their lines...and their co-stars lines.

That comes from a lot of preparation and while in some instances, Shakespeare was right, I agree with and encourage a well planned, pre meditated rehearsed selling system. And so should you. Bonus lesson here...lawyers are actually salespeople. I rest my case.

I'm Jake...
AND IN MY WORLD...
I BELIEVE THAT...

After You Don't Make A Sale,
Before You Start The Car
Figure Out Why
AND BE HONEST

That's right. Put on your big boy pants, take a deep breath and actually analyze where you went wrong. What did you miss? What did you either forget or choose not to include?

And do it before you leave the driveway. Right there. At the scene of the crime.

And when you do identify what happened, LEARN from your current failure and fix it NEXT TIME. And then, drive away with a positive attitude...ready for NEXT TIME.

I'm Jake...
AND IN MY WORLD...
I BELIEVE THAT...

You Should NEVER Talk Religion, Politics
or Why You Hope That the Steelers Lose

Absolutely, with no exceptions should you EVER talk politics, or religion.

First of all, you're not there for that. So don't think that your transparent support of whatever his existing lawn sign advertises will win you a sale. It won't. What will get you a sale is to stick with your selling system.

Secondly, your unrehearsed verbiage regarding religion or other personal matters will surely lose more sales than make them.

As for the Pittsburgh Steeler fans, charge them more. I do. A lot.

I'm Jake...
AND IN MY WORLD...
I BELIEVE THAT...

BUYING IS AN EMOTIONAL DECISION

Every once in a while, a customer that I am trying to close gets upset after my 2nd, 3rd or 4th attempt in asking for the order that they have said no to 2, 3 or 4 times.

And sometimes, they get a bit emotional. Maybe even angry.

THAT'S A GOOD THING!

Because buying is an EMOTIONAL decision.

You NEED THEM to get excited about the project, anxious to get it started or even UPSET that you are forcing them into a YES OR NO decision.

EMOTIONS are very much a part of why people buy. So make'em laugh, make'em cry, make'em desire.... and take their money.

I'm Jake...
AND IN MY WORLD...
I BELIEVE THAT...

You Should
Make New Friends
But Keep The Old
One Is Silver
The Other Is Gold

Actually this is an elementary school lesson by my third grade teacher, Mrs. Clark.. that applies to business better than any other lesson of success.

Keep learning. Keep your experience in your back pocket. Grow with technology. Practice back to basics. All the way back.

And never, never, never burn bridges.

Realize the value of yesterday and reach for tomorrow's opportunities.

I'm Jake...
AND IN MY WORLD...
I BELIEVE THAT...

You Should Take Care
OF YOU, AND YOUR FAMILY

The same way that you fine tune your business methods, your selling skills, your product line or your company profile, never forget about your family at home.

Fine tune your family situation, as well.

As Zig Ziglar always said, build not just a nice house, but a nice home.

And fine tune yourself. Exercise. Eat smart. Stay healthy.

It all matters.

I'm Jake...

AND IN MY WORLD...
I BELIEVE THAT...

You Should
SELL THE BRAND
It's Bigger Than You Are

I've never been impressed by companies or salespeople who lie to the customer by claiming that they make their own window when they don't.

When your company chooses a particular brand to sell, LEARN THAT BRAND as it is written by the makers of the product. After all, they made it.

And it's a great characteristic to show the customer your acknowledgement of experts.

Hey, wait a minute...isn't that how you want them to view you?

The brand is bigger than you are. And your endorsement of a product is a stronger message than your simply claiming that your product is the best.

I'm Jake...
AND IN MY WORLD...
I BELIEVE THAT...

The World Is Your Office

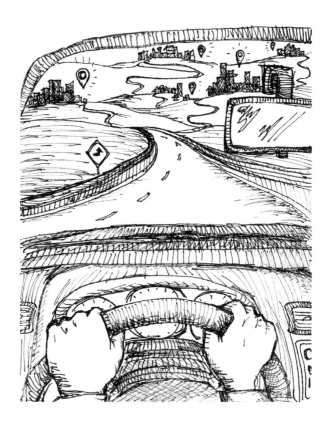

In the profession of sales, forget about the ideas of territories, profiled customers or other limitations of your efforts. Keep in mind that success may be found anywhere, so search everywhere. And the best view of your potential customer base, the foundation of your career and your potential income is the windshield.

And not the rear window. Don't look back. You're not going that way.

I'm Jake...
AND IN MY WORLD...
I BELIEVE THAT...

Before You Close,
You Need To PRE CLOSE

Just like a painter who primes before he applies the final paint finish, selling requires the step called "pre close."

After you've warmed up, measured, demonstrated your product and services... and before you give the customer the numbers (DO NOT USE THE WORDS PRICE OR INVESTMENT), direct the customer into a conversation of what colors they will pick, what options they will choose, when they're hoping to have it done and how they're looking to pay for it.

In other words, even before presenting the numbers, have the customer actually talk about doing it as though they've made a decision to do so.

Boy, is this important. And, it works. I guarantee it.

I'm Jake...

AND IN MY WORLD...

I BELIEVE THAT...

It's Better If
EVERYBODY WINS

In the process of selling a job, keep in mind that you should adopt the attitude that the outcome of the customer buying creates a definite WIN for everybody. You, the customer, your company, the installer, the factory, the marketing people...everyone. You should never settle for the idea that it's okay for anyone to get shortchanged or kept out of the success here. Every team needs a hero, sure...and every hero needs a team.

Letting everybody wins produces an all-around better outcome.

And how cool is it that you've designed that process.

Wouldn't it be great if everybody could win every day?

I think so.

I'm Jake...
AND IN MY WORLD...
I BELIEVE THAT...

When You Visit The Customer After The Job IS Installed You Earn More Than When You Sold It

Obviously when you sell a job you earn a commission and probably a relatively high one.

When you revisit the job during install or afterwards to take pictures or revisit the customer, you will earn referrals, additional business, experience that will help you sell your next job and the great feeling that you took part in helping folks. Don't stop at just your commission.

Earned commissions are spent and then they're gone. Earned experience is forever and in my world, I believe that you earn dividends.

Cool, huh?

I'm Jake...
AND IN MY WORLD...
I BELIEVE THAT...

If You Don't Ask For Referrals, They Won't Give You Any

When a customer is happy with a job or service, they're actually anxious to tell others. They're proud of what they've done and they should be. So, capitalize on that.

Simply ask them for a possible referral and all of the sudden you've grown your prospect list. Remember, it's your prospects that keep you in the game. Not the job that you just finished.

As well, don't be shy! Ask them for the referrals while you're actually selling the first job! This transfer of belief adds a lot of trust to the moment.

Whether it's now or later, if you don't ask...you probably won't get referrals. And that's dumb.

I'm Jake...
AND IN MY WORLD...
I BELIEVE THAT...

You Should
DO IT AGAIN
(It Worked The First Time)

Here's a trick question. If you sell a customer in July by offering a JULY 4th discount, can you sell that same customer another job in September by offering a discount using your Labor Day sale?

The answer is YES. It worked the first time!

If it feels good...do it again.

I'm Jake...
AND IN MY WORLD...
I BELIEVE THAT...

It is NOT Your Job
To Overcome Their Objections
It is Your Job To
HELP THEM Overcome Those Objections

That's right. IT IS NOT your job to overpower or talk your customers out of their concerns or "objections". In fact, if you do, it will counter against you. People are not impressed by you convincing them against their beliefs. Let the sale be their idea.

If anything, educate them so that they can see it the right way. If you have them speak the words of decision, they will accept those words more convincingly by listening to themselves, not you.

I'm Jake...
AND IN MY WORLD...
I BELIEVE THAT...

As A Sales Rep
You Are The Front Line Of The Company Image

While it's true that you are selling your product, your company, your services and yourself, it is also true that YOU ARE the Emcee of the entire production here. So, in many ways...YOU are what they are buying. In fact, if you have the best product, the best value, and the best company...and for whatever reason they don't like you...like, maybe you were late...then, trust me, it's over before it starts. Damn. Shame on you for striking out before you swing.

I'm Jake...
AND IN MY WORLD...
I BELIEVE THAT...

HOW TO SUCCEED IN BUSINESS
WITHOUT REALLY TRYING
Was a GREAT MOVIE
And That You Should WATCH IT

I believe that the movie stared Robert Morse who started out as a window washer. He soon got promoted to the mail room, then the office pool, appointed to the board of directors and eventually became President of the company. And all because he simply and loyally did it the company way. Pure genius. And it's easier (and smarter) to paddle the row boat the same way as everybody else.

It's also more productive, more profitable and more fun. In my training class, it's not my way, it's the company way. Come on in.

I'm Jake...

AND IN MY WORLD...

I BELIEVE THAT...

You Can't Teach Passion
Yet, You Can Learn It

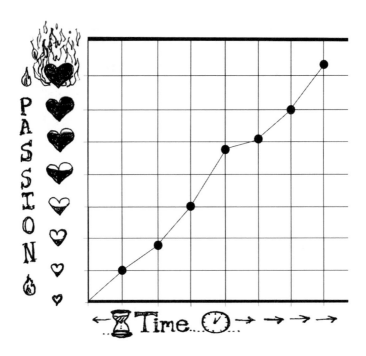

As a sales trainer, I can tell you that you can't teach passion. It is interesting, however, to watch new salespeople grow into the position of having a passion for what they do. Without a doubt, it is the best growth that anyone could ever realize and experience.

I'm Jake...

AND IN MY WORLD...

I BELIEVE THAT...

That You Should Hit'Em...
...With A Velvet Hammer

As a one call closer, I've been accused of practicing the method called the HARD SELL. And the truth of the matter is, I do in fact have every intention of GETTING THE SALE. I also do this in a SOFT sell method, which is not only non-offensive, it is also successful. A seasoned professional, Bob Hoppa once taught me that it's like tapping in a small nail with a tap hammer as opposed to a sledge hammer, I still hit them with the close. Gently, quietly and yet, still targeted. They're not offended and neither is my bank account.

I'm Jake...
AND IN MY WORLD...
I BELIEVE THAT...

Training Them To Say Yes
Is Better Than
Training Them To Say No

Keeping in mind that QUESTIONS CONTROL, also design your questions to elicit a YES answer, not a NO answer. For example, rather than ask..

"Do you want to still get up on a ladder to clean out your gutters?" (NO)

Ask..

"Would you like it if you would no longer need to get up on the ladder to clean out your gutters? (YES)

Practice this and you'll find yourself doing it all the time...and you'll realize more success..

"Do you want to keep on making a mediocre living ? " (NO)

"Would you like to make more money?" (YES)

I'm Jake...

AND IN MY WORLD...

I BELIEVE THAT...

Everyone Buys For One Of Two Reasons
They Need It
Or They Want It

Actually, it's true. People buy everything that they buy for one of those two reasons. So do you. Think about it. Either way, in selling, you should either HIT THEIR HOT BUTTONS, by either satisfying their desires or their needs. If you do, you'll sell it. If you don't, nothing else matters.

Figure Out Which One and Go for the WIN

I'm Jake...
AND IN MY WORLD...
I BELIEVE THAT...

Humor Is A Great Sales Tool
So Make'em Laugh

Always remember and never forget that buying is an emotional decision. And laughter is a POSITIVE FEEL GOOD EMOTION. So, during your sales call, at some point MAKE'EM LAUGH...Keep it respectful, appropriate and in connection with the conversation. Laughter also elicits smiles and that works too. I once read that it's advisable and a pretty good plan to, as I learned, MAKE'EM LAUGH AND TAKE THEIR MONEY".

I'm Jake...
AND IN MY WORLD...
I BELIEVE THAT...

You Should Exercise Your Body, Your Mind And
Your Selling Skills

Yep. Stay in shape. Healthy means less illness, less time off and more energy. All of which increases sales. At the same time, make time for personal relationships and enjoyment, and as a winner, win that game too. And remember to keep your selling skills sharp. In other words, take batting practice. It'll show up in the stats column.

I'm Jake...
AND IN MY WORLD...
I BELIEVE THAT...

Cal Ripken Had It Right
Before Every Game
He Warmed Up

Hall of Famer Cal Ripken taught us more than how to hit a home run.

Without taking anything away from Cal's obvious talent and athleticism, he made it look easy because he rehearsed before every game. In fact, he probably took more at bats before the game than during the game and fielded more ground balls before the game than during. Think about that. And then, become an iron man...and YES YOU CAN.

I'm Jake...
AND IN MY WORLD...
I BELIEVE THAT...

Jimmy V
Also Had It Right
NEVER GIVE UP

NEVER GIVE UP is not only a good lesson and attitude for winning the battle...but also for winning the war or even being part of the war. In other words, stay with every customer and stay focused every week, every month and every year.

And, when need be, accept defeat. As a lesson.

But while the game is on, NEVER GIVE UP. Because, in the game of selling, once it's a no sale, figure that it's over. I'm not saying be angry...you should always leave as a commercial. But know this...you'll never see them again. I guarantee it.

I'm Jake...
AND IN MY WORLD...
I BELIEVE THAT...

Yes, Sales Slumps Suck
They Are Also Great

While selling is a profession of success, it's also a profession of failure. You're not going to sell everything and in fact, if you are selling over 35%, you're a champion. (By the way, my salesmen that are using my TRAIN'EM TO SAY YES system are selling at over 55%). Join in!

In any event, 3 days without a sale is a slump. And the best way to get out of a slump is to remember your last sale AND to recognize what you maybe could have done on your last NO SALE to have been successful. Sometimes, slumps help you at least look for what's broken.

I'm Jake...
AND IN MY WORLD...
I BELIEVE THAT...

You Gotta Give Them
A Reason To Buy
Not Just Because You Want Them To Buy

Be sure to include in your selling system an offering or a discount that is only available right now. All of Macy's sales expire at midnight.

And whether or not you believe that, the customers do.

Give your customers a reason to buy now. Or they won't.

It's called the method of URGENCY.

And it is the FEAR OF LOSS by not buying tonight, thus urgency, that will often encourage the customer to lean toward the positive side of the fence. Push gently, but yes, push.

I'm Jake...
AND IN MY WORLD...
I BELIEVE THAT...

Selling Is Not Begging
In Fact, Many Sales Are Made By The
Take-Away

In other words, people often buy now because they don't want to pay more later. Or because it might be unavailable later.

Either way, decisions are based on facts, emotions and hopefully because it makes sense to buy.

It's your job to tell'em the facts and your ADVICE that it makes sense... and let the decision to buy be theirs.

I'm Jake...
AND IN MY WORLD...
I BELIEVE THAT...

By The End Of A Sales Call,
You Should Know A lot About Your Customer…
And He Should Know A Lot About You

The real purpose of a warm up is for the customer to like you. And the best way for that to happen is for you to like the customer. So, get to know him.

This should be accomplished by an absolute process. Not just the gift of gab.

I'm Jake...

AND IN MY WORLD...
I BELIEVE THAT...

When Selling, You Should Share Your Experience Not Your Opinion

They care what you know. Not what you think.

Offer advice on what you've seen, not what you envision.

Your experienced knowledge is a valuable resource for the customer to make a decision and they are lucky to have you there to help.

And be sincere.

I'm Jake...

AND IN MY WORLD...

I BELIEVE THAT...

Selling Is Hard Work And High Pay

The highest paychecks given out every Friday are the ones written to the salespeople. We are the ones working all kinds of hours, driving all over god's country, and getting home late. It's hard work. And high pay. And the pay includes some great experiences. Not just monetary stats. Take a bow...and make a bank deposit.

Welcome to the big leagues.

I'm Jake...
AND IN MY WORLD...
I BELIEVE THAT...

Sometimes Customers Need to Feel Their Pain
Before They Buy
So Ask THEM To Open Up That Window That Is Stuck

Literally. If you're inspecting or measuring a remodeling job that represents
a need , be sure that the customer touches the problem. It'll help that the pain
is current...which increases the desire to get it fixed NOW.

And maybe, if they do,

you might have a blank contract with you.

I'm Jake...

AND IN MY WORLD...

I BELIEVE THAT...

Before You Get There
They Are Making A Pact Not To Buy Today
So
Before You Go
Make A Pact To Sell

Every football team makes a huddle...a plan on either how to succeed or how to stop the other side from succeeding.

Create a winning attitude for yourself and bet on the best team.

The name of the team is YOU

I'm Jake...
AND IN MY WORLD...
I BELIEVE THAT...

If They Say NO
It May Be Because
They Don't Know
Enough

True. When they say "no", it's because they don't realize the value, the sensibility or the affordability. You might need to say it again.

I'm Jake...
AND IN MY WORLD...
I BELIEVE THAT...

If They Don't Like You
They Won't Give You Their Money
So, WARM UP
And
MEAN IT

Just like starting a car, stretching before exercise or stretching before getting out of bed....WARM UP BEFORE selling and asking for the sale.

Relationships matter here and people won't buy from who they don't like or don't know. I wouldn't, nor would you.

Warming up does both.

I'm Jake...
AND IN MY WORLD...
I BELIEVE THAT...

Your Words Are A Reflection Of Your Word

A play on words, but a real message. Sometimes its not what you say, but how you say it and what words you use to express yourself.

Offensive words are easily replaced with respectful words and cockiness is easily replaced with confidence.

Think before you talk.

Those who don't often lose the game beyond an otherwise good performance.

And No's can be easily replaced with a YES.

I'm Jake...
AND IN MY WORLD...
I BELIEVE THAT...

Every Detail Matters
So, If You Leave Something Out, It May Be The Reason
Why You Did Not Sell

In presenting your features and benefits of a product, never assume the idea that you need not talk about the screen or install process because the customer had not yet mentioned that as a hot button. That extra detail could be the selling factor or that feature just might spark a higher or additional value, which again, spells CA CHING!

I'm Jake...
AND IN MY WORLD...
I BELIEVE THAT...

Sometimes, People Just Need to Hear
How Easy It Is To Make Their Dreams Affordable.

KISS stands for Keep It Simple Stupid. When selling, avoid complicated details that the customer will not only not understand, but will block out their conception of simplicity. People like simplicity. And, sensibility. Highlight both.

I'm Jake...
AND IN MY WORLD...
I BELIEVE THAT...

Yes, You Are Building Their Dream

Picture this. When selling a deck, use driveway stakes and fluorescent string to lay out the size and location. You will see the customers stand in the middle and sometimes move the patio furniture to the staked area. And when they do, they become excited. Its their dream. And if they don't buy, ask them to help take down the strings and stakes. That takes away their dream, and they become sad.

Highlight and let them live their dream. And you can dream about your bank account.

I'm Jake...
AND IN MY WORLD...
I BELIEVE THAT...

If Your Co Worker Tells You How Bad Everything Is Over Lunch, You Should Stop Having Lunch With Him

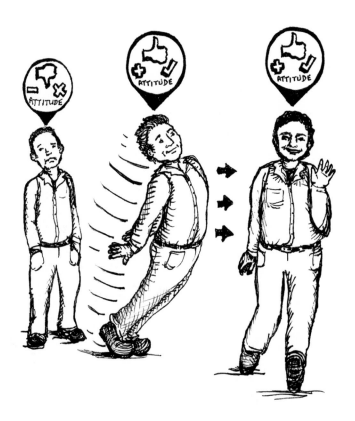

In other words, stay away from negativity. It's contagious, its only purpose is to highlight failure and you might just find it to be more fun to have lunch with someone with a positive attitude. And, next time, you can also afford to buy him lunch. Well, actually, you should be buying somebody else lunch. Get the message?

I'm Jake...
AND IN MY WORLD...
I BELIEVE THAT...

You Should
Work Hard
AND
Work Smart

Working hard means working as much as you can and trying to feel like you just worked out at the gym at the end of the day. Working smart means skipping no processes of the system, not making false statements or promises and selling clean jobs, completing clean paperwork and feeling good about being a part of a win-win process.

Do both.

I'm Jake...
AND IN MY WORLD...
I BELIEVE THAT...

RESPECT
Matters
In Every Direction

Absolutely. Respect shouldn't have to be earned. Respect everyone from the start. It could be lost, like bad credit, but everyone deserves it from the start.

And that includes every customer, every installer, every manufacturer, every secretary and office worker and every family member.

And when you give respect, you get respect.

If not, then you don't deserve respect.

I'm Jake...
AND IN MY WORLD...
I BELIEVE THAT...

IF YOU'VE GOTTA HAVE A TOUGH CONVERSATION...
DO IT FIRST THING IN THE MORNING

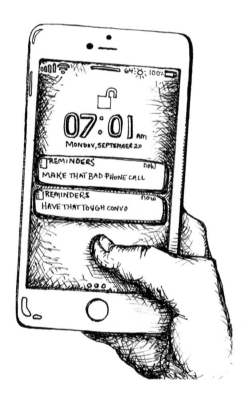

Wanna have a good day? We all do.

Simple. Get those bad chores out of the way as soon as you wake up. Procrastinating until later will work on your mind, your mental strength and your performance.

So plan your day wisely. And procrastination is a bad plan.

I'm Jake...
AND IN MY WORLD...
I BELIEVE THAT...

Every Team Has Hero And
Every Hero Has A Team

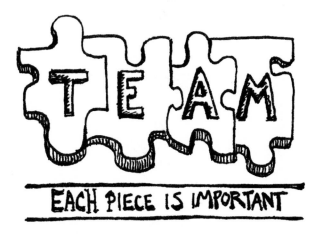

Sure, it's great to be confident and sometimes, a little cocky. But never think that success is all about you. Without the lead, you have no customers to sell. Without the customers, the company has no jobs to do. Without jobs, the installers have no work. Without work, the company has no income. And, oh yeah, without income, you can't get paid. Team is a great concept.

I'm Jake...
AND IN MY WORLD...
I BELIEVE THAT...

You Work
FOR YOUR COMPANY
Not
AT YOUR COMPANY

As an employee, no matter what your job description is, it's important to be a company advocate and a company cheerleader. Believe in the fact that whoever is buying from your company is fortunate to be buying from a good company with a good product line. And you should believe that you are fortunate to be a part of their plan. And if you ask me, you are.

I'm Jake...

AND IN MY WORLD...

I BELIEVE THAT...

YOU SHOULD ROOT FOR THE HOME TEAM
AND THAT INCLUDES YOUR TEAMMATES

At every sales meeting, my reps talk about their successes that week...and not to boast or to play gamesmanship against another rep.

In fact, we applaud him. And we're happy for him. And we mean it. Being a great player on a lousy team is not a good position to be in. It's far better to be a great player on a winning team.

I'm Jake...
AND IN MY WORLD...
I BELIEVE THAT...

If Anyone Asks You What You Do For A Living...
Don't say..."I Sell..." Say, "I Help People"...

Because guess what. You do.

I'm Jake...

AND IN MY WORLD...

I BELIEVE THAT...

THE BEST FEELING IN THE WORLD
IS WHEN
YOU LOVE THE GAME BEYOND THE SCORE

Over the years, I've made a lot of money in the business of selling.

More than many doctors, first responders, teachers or others who deserve high pay. And the reason they do what they do is because of what they get beyond their paycheck. The satisfaction of enjoying their careers.

And so do I. In fact, I LOVE IT.

And If you're lucky....well, so should you.

By the way, I learned this lesson from my son who played college lacrosse. It was him that taught me that he loved playing every game and that the score (the paycheck) was secondary.

Please feel free to contact JAKE by email, phone or web site for a FREE initial consultation and additional information regarding consulting, speaking engagements and training.

website: theworldofjakebelieve.com
email: theworldofjakebelieve@gmail.com
phone number: 410-977-5746